CORNISH WALKS

WALKING IN THE FOWEY AREA

GW00578193

LIZ HURLEY

MUDLARK'S PRESS

First Edition, 2018

ISBN: 9780993218040

All maps in this publication are reproduced from Ordnance Survey 1:25,000 maps, with the permission of The Controller of Her Majesty's Stationery Office, Crown copyright.

A CIP catalogue record for this book is available from the British Library.

Mudlarks' Press

www.hurleybooks.co.uk

CONTENTS

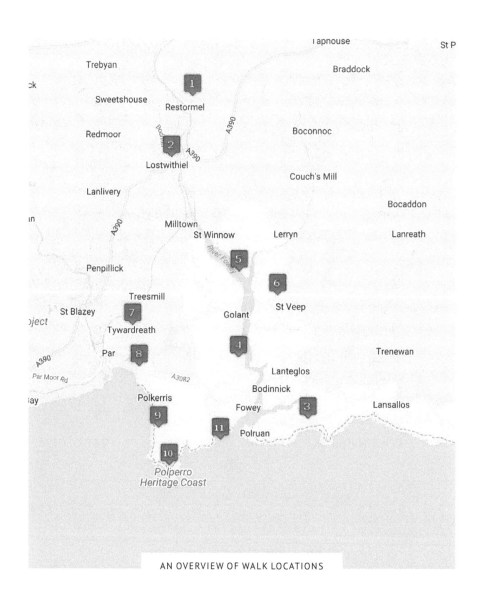

AN OVERVIEW OF WALK LOCATIONS

INTRODUCTION

Welcome to Cornish Walks. This series is designed to help you explore an area in greater depth and will feature a wide range of walks.

Nearly all the walks are circular so you can walk in either direction, although the guide only explains the route one way. If you want a longer walk, just retrace your footsteps for a change of scenery. Some of the shorter walks have a neighbouring walk that they can be linked to. I have said at the start of a walk if this is an option.

If you do all the walks and their extensions in this book, you will have walked almost 60 miles. You will have travelled past Norman and Tudor castles, walked the paths of ancient saints, followed streams and rivers down to the sea and beyond. You will have stood in the place of lost estates and hidden wonders and hopefully also spotted some Cornish wildlife as well.

As these are largely countryside / coastal walks, the majority will not be suitable for wheelchairs or buggies.

I have also taken into account walking with dogs. I walk with two Spaniels myself and find them the most challenging of dogs, so I use them as my benchmark. When I say challenging, I mean that they enjoy being off the lead and roaming. Therefore, I tend not to take them on walks where there is traffic, cliffs or a lot of livestock. If I do, they are on leads. For the same reason, I like car parks that end near water!

Walks 3, 8 & 11 are brilliant for dogs, although there will be some on-lead parts on the coast path sections of 8 & 11. Walk 5 is also excellent if, when you get to St Winnow, you simply turn around and head back again, avoiding the top fields.

Throughout the guide are snippets of information regarding the landscape around you and generally a recommendation for a good place to eat. Each walk also features links to further information and a link to a photo gallery of sights from the walk.

At the back of the book, there are some added extras, to enhance your walks. Ranging from recipes and recommended reads to an explanation of how the tides work. I hope that you find them, and the rest of the book, enjoyable.

INSTRUCTIONS

COUNTRY CODE

• Respect the people who live and work in the countryside. Respect private property, farmland and all rural environments.

• Do not interfere with livestock, machinery and crops.

• Respect and, where possible, protect all wildlife, plants and trees.

• When walking, use the approved routes and keep as closely as possible to them.

• Take special care when walking on country roads.

• Leave all gates as you find them and do not interfere with or damage any gates, fences, walls or hedges.

• Guard against all risks of fire, especially near forests.

• Always keep children closely supervised while on a walk.

• Do not walk the Ways in large groups and always maintain a low profile.

• Take all litter home - leaving only footprints behind.

• Keep the number of cars used to the minimum and park carefully to avoid blocking farm gateways or narrow roads.

• Minimise impact on fragile vegetation and soft ground.

• Take heed of warning signs - they are there for your protection.

Dogs

• All of the walks in this book are suitable for dogs on leads. There are a few walks with stiles that may prove troublesome depending on the size and athleticism of your companion. Some walks are particularly good for dogs as they can be safely off the lead for large portions of the walk.

The Countryside Code states that:

- By law, you must keep your dog under effective control so that it does not disturb or scare farm animals or wildlife. On most areas of open country and common land, known as 'access land' you must keep your dog on a short lead between 1 March and 31 July, and all year round near farm animals.

- You do not have to put your dog on a lead on public paths, as long as it is under close control. But as a general rule, keep your dog on a lead if you cannot rely on its obedience. By law, farmers are entitled to destroy a dog that injures or worries their animals.

- If livestock chase you and your dog, it is safer to let your dog off the lead – don't risk getting hurt by trying to protect it.

- Take particular care that your dog doesn't scare sheep and lambs or wander where it might disturb birds that nest on the ground and other wildlife – eggs and young will soon die without protection from their parents.

- Everyone knows how unpleasant dog mess is and it can cause infections – so always clean up after your dog and get rid of the mess responsibly. Also make sure your dog is wormed regularly to protect it, other animals and people.

- At certain times, dogs may not be allowed on some areas of access land or may need to be kept on a lead. Please follow any signs.

Cattle

- If you find yourself in a field of suddenly wary cattle, move away as carefully and quietly as possible, and if you feel threatened by cattle then let go of your dog's lead and let it run free rather than try to protect it and endanger yourself. The dog will outrun the cows, and it will also outrun you.

- Those without canine companions should follow similar advice: move away calmly, do not panic and make no sudden noises. Chances are the cows will leave you alone once they establish that you pose no threat.

- If you walk through a field of cows and there happen to be calves, think twice; if you can, go another way and avoid crossing fields

Tides

- There is a useful explanation on tides at the back of the book.

GUIDE TO THE LEGEND

Before heading off for a walk read the description first. You may discover issues with it. Cows, amount of stiles, mud etc. Then have a look at a map, not the little one provided with the walk, to get a proper feel for the direction of the walk.

LENGTH: This has been calculated using a range of GPS tracking devices.
EFFORT: Easy to Challenging. These descriptions are only in relation to each other in this book. Every walk has at least one hill in it; not everyone finds hills easy. Challenging, this is for the hardest walks in the book, it will be based on effort and duration. However, nothing in here is particularly tortuous.
TERRAIN: If it's been raining a lot, please assume that footpaths will be muddy. Coast paths tend to be a bit better, near villages they tend to be a bit worse.
FOOTWEAR: I usually walk in walking boots, trainers or ridge sole welling-tons. Except for village walks, smart shoes, sandals, heels or flip flops are unsuitable. Crocs are always unsuitable.*
LIVESTOCK: It is possible that you won't encounter any livestock on a walk that mentions them. Please read the Countryside Code section, on how to avoid them if you do.
PARKING: Postcode for sat nav given. Be aware Cornwall is not always kind to sat navs, have a road map to hand and check you know where you are heading before you set off.
WCs: Due to council cuts, lots of loos are now closed or run by local parishes with seasonal opening hours. If they are an essential part of your walk, check online first. Lots are now coin operated.
CAFÉ / PUB: Local recommendations. Always check ahead, some will have seasonal opening hours.
OS MAP: This will be the largest scale available for the area.
BRIEF DESCRIPTION: Just a quick outline of the walk.

DIRECTIONS: If I say, "going up the road" up or down means there is a slope. If I refer to North or SW, you will need a compass. Most smartphones have built-in compasses. It won't be essential as other directions will be given, but it will be an aide. Especially in woodland where there are few other clues.

IN SIZE OF SCALE, LARGEST TO SMALLEST: Road, lane, unmade road, track, trail, path. Although some of the smaller descriptions are interchangeable.

OPTIONS: Several of the walks have options or alternate routes to avoid mud, cattle, seasonal access etc. You only need to choose one option, but please read the whole section first . It will help to rule out any confusion.

THINGS CHANGE: Trees fall down, posts get broken, signs become obscured, footpaths can be closed for repair. Do not be alarmed if you can't see a marker.

TIDES: Occasionally I refer to the fact that a high spring tide might block the path, this tends to only last for about an hour, every few months, in the early morning or evening. You are unlikely to be hindered but it is worth pointing out.

LINKS: In the print book, I have shortened very long hyperlinks for ease of typing and I have left easy hyperlinks as they are. In the e-book they are active.

*JOKE**

**NOT REALLY :D

1

RESTORMEL CASTLE – LANHYDROCK HOUSE

LENGTH: 8.5 miles
EFFORT: Moderate to challenging, simply due to length and hills
TERRAIN: Lanes, cycle paths, footpaths
FOOTWEAR: Walking boots, trainers
LIVESTOCK: Sheep
PARKING: Lanhydrock NT car park. PL30 5AD
WCs: Lanhydrock / Duchy Nurseries / Bodmin Parkway station
CAFÉ / PUB: Lanhydrock / Duchy Nurseries
OS MAP: 107

BRIEF DESCRIPTION: A great day out, walking through the ages with lots of lovely views and impressive architecture.

Elevation Profile

LANHYDROCK GATEHOUSE

DIRECTIONS:

1. Park in the *Lanhydrock Estate* main car park. Head towards the house, and as you leave the car park you will come to a road. Instead of crossing it towards the house, turn left and walk up the road with the cricket pavilion on your left. At the T-junction, cross the road and enter the woods. You are now on a large unmade road, this is a very popular cycle trails area so keep an eye out for lots of bikes. Head forwards and take a right-hand

Lanhydrock Estate: Lanhydrock is the perfect country house and estate, with the feel of a wealthy but unpretentious family home. After a devastating fire in 1881 the Jacobean house was refurbished in high-Victorian style, with the best in country house design & planning and the latest mod-cons. Beyond the house, the gardens and further estate grounds are

path leading downhill. This will have a National Trust post, with a green oak leaf, a yellow arrow and a no bikes sign.

2.   It is about a 10 / 15 minutes walk downhill. When you get to the bottom head through the gate, cross the road and into the Lanhydrock Estate grounds. Cross over the formal path and take the path following the stream; keep it on your right and walk down to the river. When you get to the river, turn left and follow it upriver. The path rejoins the formal path and turns right. Walk between the metal railings, over the river and continue all the way to Bodmin Parkway railway station.

3.   As you walk into the car park, you need to turn sharp right towards an industrial estate. When you get to the gates for the estate, stay on the drive as it veers to the right. The road becomes increasingly unmade, as you get halfway along the very long building on your left you need to take an unsigned footpath to your right. The path heads straight down to the railway line and there are some storage buildings on your right. Turn left and walk along the path. Go through a five-bar gate and continue along the path. When you get to the kissing gate, you are now walking through a private garden. Head towards their drive and then walk along it away from the house. Follow the drive all the way to the road.

beautiful to explore, and this walk winds through a lot of them free of charge. The newly developed cycle trails are also worth exploring. Dating from the seventeenth century, the main gatehouse escaped the ravages of the fire. This makes it one of the few remaining features of the previous great house.

Restormel Castle: The great thirteenth century circular shell-keep of Restormel still encloses the principal rooms of the castle in remarkably good condition. It stands on an earlier Norman mound surrounded by a deep dry ditch, atop a high spur beside the River Fowey. Twice visited by the Black Prince, it finally saw action during the Civil War in 1644. It commands fantastic views and is a favourite picnic spot. When you visit, keep an eye out for 'Tetraphasis Obscurus', the 'Black Pheasant' that you can spot in the castle grounds and nearby woodland. This is a haven for wildlife and birds with beautiful spring flowers and plants all year round.

4.   At the road, turn left. Start walking uphill, take the right-hand turning to Lostwithiel and continue walking uphill. Eventually, the road turns right to the "Duchy of Cornwall Nursery and Café". This whole section, from where the path joins the road to the Duchy turning is about 1.5 miles. As you walk under the pylon lines, you are just about at the turning. This is a quiet road with lovely high views.

5.   At the turning, head right, this lane is much smaller and finally downhill. As you look to your right across the valley, you can see *Restormel Castle* nestling on the hillside. Continue down the lane until you get to the driveway for the *Duchy Nurseries*. Take the footpath opposite the driveway on your right. Go through the small gate marked "EH Restormel Castle". The path zigzags all the way downhill and is well signed.

6.   At the bottom go through the five-bar gate and follow the path along to the railway bridge and then over the river bridge as well. Go through another gate and then follow the path as it skirts around *Restormel Manor*. Go through the next gate and then walk forward towards the estate buildings until you get to a T-junction.

7.   If you want to visit the castle, turn left and follow the signs, returning to this point afterwards. It is very impressive,

BODMIN PARKWAY FOOTBRIDGE

Duchy Nurseries: This is an excellent garden centre but the café is even better. Absolutely stop here and treat yourself to a really tasty menu freshly cooked with local ingredients.

Restormel Manor: Restormel Manor is approximately 500 years old and sits on the site of the ancient Holy Trinity Chapel. It is one of the Duchy of Cornwall's favourite buildings and you will see the Standard flying above the buildings. The manor itself now acts as private holiday accommodation and is often used by the Royal family when visiting the area.

Duchy of Cornwall: Along with Lancashire, Cornwall is the only duchy remaining in Britain. The Duke of Cornwall is also the Prince of Wales and heir to the British throne. Unlike Lancashire, the Cornish Duchy has developed historically, unusual legal amendments have created a special position within the UK. In 2014, the UK government announced that the "*proud*

being a rare example of a Norman circular castle, but is only opened seasonally.

8.　At the car park by the *Duchy of Cornwall* estate office, turn right and stick to the road for the next mile, this is a flat and very quiet road. When it bears left, go through the gate and carry on walking forward on the road. This will make more sense when you see it.

9.　Walk past the water treatment centre and continue walking forward as the road turns into a track in a field.

history, unique culture, and distinctive language of Cornwall will be fully recognised under European rules for the protection of national minorities."

RESTORMEL MANOR

Continue through the field until you get to the maroon gate. Pass through and you are now back in the Lanhydrock Estate.

10. Turn right and head down towards the river. When you get to the river, turn left and follow it upstream until you get to a footbridge. Cross over the river and continue upstream until you get to the road.

11. Turn left onto the road and cross over *Respryn Bridge*, walk past the car park on your right and then take the left-hand turning up to Lanhydrock. Follow this path through the first gatehouse and up the ornamental drive right up to the very ornate main *gatehouse*. Turn right before this second gatehouse and follow the road uphill. This leads back to your car park.

Respryn Bridge:
Respryn Bridge is a five-arched mediaeval bridge spanning the River Fowey in the parish of Lanhydrock. The place name indicates a ford here before the bridge was built, carrying an ancient trackway between Bodmin and Looe: traces of which have been identified as a hollow way running north-westwards through Cutmadoc and Colgear Plantation in Lanhydrock Park. The first part of the name Respryn contains the Cornish place-name element rid meaning 'ford'. Documentary evidence indicates a chapel of St Martin, on the St Winnow side of the river in the twelfth century. This predated the bridge and served the fording point. By 1300, however, there was a bridge here.

LINKS:

Duchy Nurseries Opening Times http://www.duchyofcornwallnursery.co.uk/
Lanhydrock – National Trust https://www.nationaltrust.org.uk/lanhydrock
Respryn Bridge http://bit.ly/2HXf7V9
Restormel Castle http://bit.ly/2GbrrUK

PHOTO ALBUM:

https://flic.kr/s/aHsmeDgEFW

2

LOSTWITHIEL LOOP

LENGTH: 3.5 miles
EFFORT: Initial steep hill, after that, easy and downhill
TERRAIN: Lanes and footpaths
FOOTWEAR: Any
LIVESTOCK: Some possibility of sheep
PARKING: Lostwithiel community centre car park. PL22 0HE
WCs: Lostwithiel
CAFÉ / PUB: Lots to choose from in Lostwithiel
OS MAP: 107

BRIEF DESCRIPTION: An absolutely lovely walk up hills and down through tree tunnels, following the paths of streams and rivers back into the once powerful and ancient town of Lostwithiel.

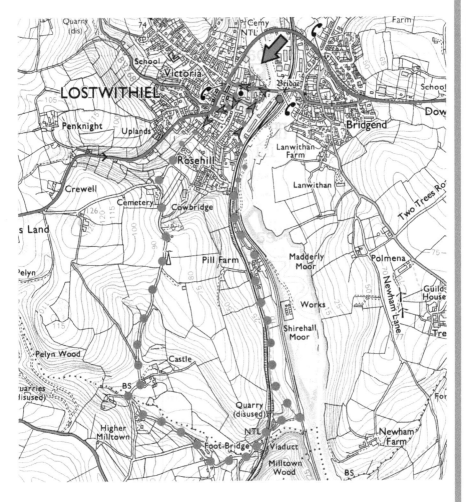

Elevation Profile

160ft

0.0ft

| 0.0mi | 0.62mi | 1.2mi | 1.9mi | 2.5mi | 3.1mi | 3.3mi |

DUCHY PALACE

DIRECTIONS:

1. From the lower end of the main *Lostwithiel* car park follow the alleyway into the town. As you come out onto a road, turn right up towards the church. Turn left down Church Lane then cross the road and continue along the lane. Take the first right and head along South Street toward the main A390. Turn left at the main road, heading uphill and then take the left-hand turning up Castle Hill, passing Hillside Gardens on your left. Castle Hill is a long steep hill, the first half of it being very steep. However, after that, the rest of the walk is rewarding and more importantly, downhill.

Lostwithiel:
Lostwithiel's history as the former capital of Cornwall, albeit 700 years ago, means the ancient buildings and narrow alleyways around the town prove to be an intriguing place to visit and as you'll discover there are lots of tiny passages and ancient granite buildings.

2. Head up Castle Hill for a quarter of a mile until the road widens, and there is a clear turning to the right. Stick to the road as it veers left. It continues to climb, but the ascent is far more gradual, after another quarter of a mile you reach a large antennae mast, this is the highest point of the walk.

3. The road begins to head downhill and becomes heavily wooded, at times the trees and steep banks appear to create a tunnel. After a while, a small stream starts to run alongside the road, keep heading downhill into the hamlet of Castle. Continue along the road as it veers right heading over a stone bridge and on towards the hamlet of Milltown. As you reach Milltown walk down through the hamlet until you get to the bottom with a post box to your right and a No Through Road sign to your left.

4. Walk along the no through road and at the end take the stone clapper bridge over the stream on your left. Now take the footpath heading forwards into the wood. Walk along the path, passing under the enormous railway viaduct, and then the path leads into open meadow with the River Fowey flowing on the right.

5. Walk along the lower edge of the meadow, then head through a second meadow, keeping the railway line and river to your right. The path is clear to follow

Duchy Palace: The Stannary Palace, also known as the Duchy Palace, circa 1265–1300, was a complex of buildings constructed by the Earls of Cornwall as the centre of their administration. The exchequer hall is reputed to be the oldest non-ecclesiastical building in Cornwall. As you have a look at the building's walls, you can see evidence of previous occupants. There are the three feathers for the Prince of Wales, possibly from 1353, there is the earliest recorded Duchy Coat of Arms from 1650, featuring the 15 bezants, these look like round balls, and then there are the Masonic symbols indicating later masonic occupation.

Lostwithiel Bridge: The Lostwithiel Bridge marks the reach of the river's tidal limit; the sea is 6 miles downstream. It was built in the 1300s, with nine arches and is a scheduled ancient monument.

LOSTWITHIEL BRIDGE

ANCIENT LANES

as you head towards the trees opposite. Pass through a gate in the top left corner of the field and take another woodland footpath. At one point the path runs along the main London train line, so be warned, it might suddenly get quite loud.

6.   The path opens out into Pill Farm, follow the lane down through the various farm buildings and continue walking. You are now walking between two railway lines, the mainline is to your left and the private clay-train line is to your right. The lane ends at a T-junction with both left and right each heading under a railway line. Turn right and head into Coulson Park. Turn left and walk through the park until you get to Quay Street.

7.   Walk along the Quay, passing the ancient *Duchy Palace* on your left and follow the road around to the right and on towards the famous *Lostwithiel Bridge*. At the bridge, turn left onto North Street, and your entrance to the car park is a few hundred yards up on your right.

LINKS:

Lostwithiel https://www.lostwithiel.org.uk/
Lostwithiel Bridge http://bit.ly/2GQtHyA
The Duchy Palace http://bit.ly/2HVaWt8

PHOTO ALBUM:

https://flic.kr/s/aHsmbwbGxA

3

FOWEY HALL WALK

LENGTH: 3.5 miles
EFFORT: Moderate
TERRAIN: Footpath
FOOTWEAR: Trainers, boots
LIVESTOCK: Some potential but alternate route available
PARKING: Caffa Mill car park. The walk starts at this point, but you may want to park in the car park on the edge of the village. In August driving to the starting point can be tricky and also full. PL23 1DF
WCs: Fowey
CAFÉ / PUB: Fowey
OS MAP: 107

BRIEF DESCRIPTION: A beautiful and popular walk, loved since at least the Tudor times. This version offers a slightly different path, adding a ruined mediaeval chapel, a stunning ancient church and a chance to paddle and maybe spot a seal or two. You even get two boat rides!

You do need to pay for the boat taxis, sailings are regular but check their websites in the Links at the end of the walk.

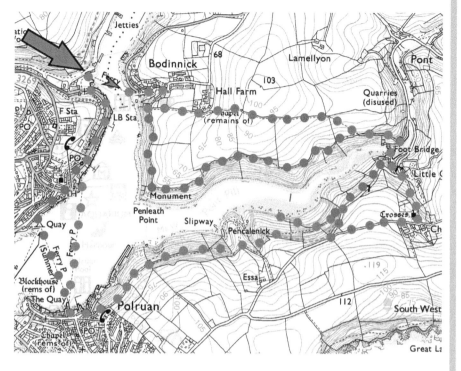

Elevation Profile

DIRECTIONS:

1. Start at the Caffa Mill car park and take the *ferry* over to Bodinnick, enjoying the *sights from the water*. Stepping off, walk uphill passing the Old Ferry Inn and some large anchors on your left. Continue up past St Johns Church on your right, and just after the Old School House you will see a signpost for the start of the *Hall Walk*, heading towards Pont and Polruan.

2. As you reach the large granite war memorial with a sword engraved on it, you now have two options.

OPTION ONE

To continue along the regular Hall Walk stick to this path. This will take in the Q Memorial on Penleath Point with lovely views down the River Fowey, the path is clear, level and mainly wooded. There is no chance of cattle on this route and is great for dogs to have a roam. We re-join Option Two, just above Pont, at Step 6.

OPTION TWO – RECOMMENDED OPTION

Chance of cattle & steep hill but open fields stunning views and a ruined chapel.

Hall Walk: Originally a promenade for Hall Manor, built just above Bodinnick in the thirteenth century, it was mentioned by Richard Carew in 1585 as *"evenly levelled, to serve for bowling, floored with sand, for soaking up the rayne, closed with two thorne hedges, and banked with sweete senting flowers: It wideneth to a sufficient breadth, for the march of five or six in front, and extendeth, to not much lesse, then halfe a London mile .....and is converted on the foreside, into platformes, for the planting of Ordinance, and the walkers sitting; and on the back part, into Summer houses, for their more private retrait and recreation."* It stopped at Penleath Point where the Q Memorial stands. Nowadays, the walk extends around to Polruan.

3.   Just before the war memorial, take the stile on your left. There is a little gate for dogs as well. The signpost says Pont via Hall Farm, 1 mile. Walk along the left-hand edge of the field heading up to the metal gate in the corner. There may be cattle in these fields. This whole section is well signed with yellow arrows on round discs.

4.   Go through the gate and into a farm drive, walk uphill, just as you clear the farm buildings you will get to the ruined *Hall Chapel* on your left. You are welcome to enter and explore but be aware of all the scaffolding and keep dogs on a short lead.

5.   Return to the concrete drive and continue uphill. At the top the drive ends at three fields. The views to your right are spectacular. Now head into the middle field and walk along the left-hand edge, keep an eye out for the yellow arrows. Through another metal gate and continue along the left-hand edge. From up here, you can see *Lanteglos Church* tower to your right.

6.   Just as you get to the next metal gate there is a lovely example of vertical slate hedging and a sheep stile. Go through the gate and now head diagonally downhill across the field towards the woods. Head toward a tree stump in the middle of the field and beyond it in

Hall Chapel: "The chapel, dedicated to St John the Baptist is recorded in 1374. It belonged to the Mohun family, whose mansion lay to the north and was also probably used for public worship. The antiquarians of the 19th century recorded its subsequent re-use as a barn and granary. Henderson made a full record of it in 1924 and noted that during the conversion the east window had been removed and this wall rebuilt to accommodate the cart doorway and a second storey loft had been inserted. He also noted the oak cradle roof was almost perfect and said an enclosure to the south had contained a cemetery." Historic England.

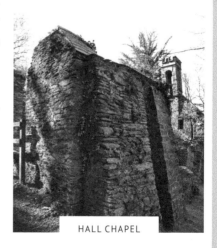

HALL CHAPEL

the corner of the field is the next gate and coffen stile. This is where we rejoin Option One.

7.   Go through the wooden gate and follow the path left, downhill to *Pont* you can catch glimpses below on your right. At the T-junction, the signpost says Polruan, take this, turning right and heading down into Pont. Walk across the river and head forwards passing the large buildings, keeping an eye out for a wooden National Trust signpost at knee level pointing the way. Walk past Pont Creek Cottage and take the obvious path uphill with the stream on your left.

8.   Continue up the path to *Lanteglos Church*, ignoring the right-hand path to Polruan. It's 370 yards uphill, but it really is

i **Lanteglos Church:** Legend has it that St Wyllow was beheaded for reasons unknown. Unhappy with his predicament he picked up his head, walked half a mile and placed it down by a bridge, indicating that this was to be his final resting place. Lanteglos Church was then built on that spot. This is a grade one listed church with evidence of Norman features in its tower arches and doorway. Everywhere you look are unusual features, from the very ornate and unusual stone cross with a lantern head, to the wooden wagon roof and painted wooden panelling.

LANTEGLOS CHURCH

a special church, I've never seen so much original woodwork inside a parish church. If this doesn't appeal, take the right-hand path to Polruan. Halfway up the path to the church, it crosses a small road, head over and continue up, with the stream again on your left.

9. Having explored the church and graveyard head out onto the road in front, and walk right. This is a very quiet country lane and is festooned with flowers in spring and summer. At the T-junction turn right and walk downhill, after a short while there is a wooden gate on your left. Go through the gate and turn left onto the footpath, which immediately splits. Take the right-hand fork heading downhill, it is signed Polruan 1¼ mile. This is where we rejoin the Hall Walk, continue with the river below on your right.

10. For another pleasant diversion, you can take the next right-hand footpath down to *Pont Creek* for a chance to paddle and keep an eye out for seals in the river. When you are ready to continue, carry along the path uphill, this return path is quite steep, but there is a bench at the top, should you feel the need for a quick moment of contemplation.

11. Turn right and continue along on the main Hall Walk. Just after the bench, the path crosses a small lane. Continue along the path keeping an eye out for a

Pont and Pont Creek: Pont Creek is also known as Pont Pill. Pill being derived from the Cornish word, pyll, meaning creek. Many of the smaller creeks are called pills. Pont is an old word for ferryboat, usually a chain boat. It's also French for bridge. Both origins of the word seem appropriate. The large buildings on either side of the river are lime kilns and until the last century, this was a busy little quay. Pont creek itself is a great place to sit and spot wildlife including the odd seal.

Sights from the water: As you head out on the Bodinnick ferry, to your left you can see Fowey's deep water docks, massive cruise liners can sometimes be seen in the water as well as giant tankers. These make for a very dramatic sight as they tower above the buildings below. Ahead of you, the blue and white building is Ferryside, once Daphne du Maurier's home.

Heading back across the water from Polruan you can see, to your far left, Henry VIII's naval defences at St Catherine's Castle,

pillbox on your left just before another bench. You are now above Polruan. As you head down into the village, you walk down a flight of steps, then turn right and head down another flight, keep heading down until you get to the quay. The ferry leaves from the slipway by the public loos.

12. The ferry either goes to the Whitehouse Pier or the Town Quay, whichever one you get on when you disembark turn right and follow the road through the town, it will be a slightly longer walk if you get dropped off at Whitehouse Pier. There are great sights from the river. Follow the main road out of Fowey, walking along the river until you get back to the Caffa Mill car park or wherever you started your walk.

then a large crenellated house Point Neptune, built for William Rashleigh in 1862. Looking toward the centre of the village you can see Fowey Church, the start and end of the Saints Way. Beside it stands the impressive crenellated Place House, built in the fifteenth century and home to the Treffrys a powerful family and large landowners.

Pillbox: The Polruan pillbox is of the FW3/22 variety, hexagonal in shape, and was built for the second world war. "A Pillbox is a simple structure made of concrete used to protect and shelter soldiers and machine gun crews from incoming bullets, shrapnel, and shell splinters; while allowing them to return fire." Homefront Legacy.

POLRUAN FERRY

BOAT STORE

LINKS:

Bodinnick Ferry http://www.ctomsandson.co.uk/bodinnick-ferry/
Hall Chapel http://bit.ly/2GilQfc
Pillboxes http://bit.ly/2u69yBK
Polruan Ferry http://www.ctomsandson.co.uk/polruan-ferry/
Q Memorial http://www.quillercouch.co.uk/q-and-fowey-2/
Types of Stiles http://bit.ly/2G2bL2X

PHOTO ALBUM:

https://flic.kr/s/aHsm7etvP9

4
...

WALKING WITH SAINTS, DRAGONS, LOVERS AND KINGS

LENGTH: 5.5 miles
(+1.5 if you do the Castle Dore extension)
EFFORT: Challenging, often muddy. Several big hills
TERRAIN: Fields, paths, lanes. About half the walk is on tarmac
FOOTWEAR: Walking boots. Wellies essential after heavy rain
LIVESTOCK: Potential for cattle in some fields on the Castle Dore extension
PARKING: Passage Lane car park, Fowey, PL23 1DY. This postcode covers a wide area, make sure you are heading to the car park, not the housing estate
WCs: Fowey
CAFÉ / PUB: Fowey
OS MAP: 107

BRIEF DESCRIPTION: A fabulous walk through Cornish folklore and history. It is a challenging walk along the initial stretch of the Saints Way but well worth the effort. An extension is available to visit Castle Dore, a well preserved ancient hillfort and one of the sites of the legend of Tristan and Iseult. Some of the hidden lanes can be very muddy.

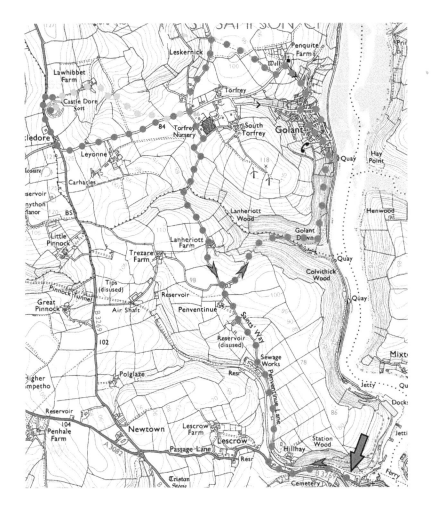

Elevation Profile

330ft					
160ft					
0.0mi	1.2mi	2.5mi	3.7mi	5.0mi	6.2mi	7.0mi

29

SAINTS WAY

DIRECTIONS:

1. From the Passage Lane car park, head onto the road and turn right. This is a busy and narrow road without footpaths; please take care. Walk along the road for just under half a mile until you get to Penventinue Lane on your right. Follow this lane for about a mile uphill until it appears to end. There are some dilapidated buildings, and the Saints Way continues in the right-hand corner of the clearing. It is well signed as the *Saints Way Path*. Penventinue Lane is long and uphill all the way. By the time you get to the top, you will be wondering why you brought a coat.

Sawmills Studio: Sawmills Studio is the site of a music studio that has hosted the likes of Robert Plant, Stone Roses, Oasis, Muse and Jessie J. It is still an active studio so if you hear music, you might be listening to the next best-selling album.

2.   The path now travels between fields, through a kissing-gate and into a large wooded valley. During spring, the wood is full of bluebells and wild garlic. Take the left-hand footpath that heads down to a small creek. This is an idyllic setting and is home to *Sawmills Studio*, but it's also private property so please stick to the footpath.

3.   The path heads over a wooden bridge and continues up the other side of the wooded valley. In winter there are stunning views down over the Fowey River. This section of the path can be very muddy. It drops down into the small village of Golant. As it joins the road continue forward, then turn right and head down to the water's edge. Turn left along the river passing the Fisherman's Arms. Given Golant's history of apple orchards, a pint of cider would be a good call at this point. Continue along the waterfront and head uphill away from the river. Just after the red brick building, the village Reading Rooms, turn right onto School Hill.

4.   School Hill is an unforgiving climb, halfway up, the road forks, take the left-hand fork and continue up the road, which is now Church Hill, it just gets steeper. Eventually, you get to *St Sampson Church*, head through the *Church Gates* with the names *Tristan and Iseult* on it and rest.

i **Tristan and Iseult:** The love story of Tristan and Iseult has been performed over the centuries; most notable examples are Wagner's opera *Tristan and Isolde* or the Kneehigh Theatre's production of *Tristan and Yseult*. There are many variations of the tale, and all are complicated, but the bare bones are that Tristan is sent by his Uncle Mark, King of the Cornish, to escort his new bride, Iseult, from Ireland. On the journey home, they accidentally drink the love potion destined for Mark and Iseult and fall in love. She marries the King but remains in love with Tristan, and they continue to see each other. They are discovered and Mark is furious. Whichever variation you follow it is the basic love triangle and people die in tragic circumstances.

Other parts of the legend feature in Walk 5, Ethy Woods.

CATARACTS ABOVE SAWMILLS

5.   After a rest and explore, leave via the upper gate and continue along the road. After about 100 yards look out for the footpath on your right-hand side. It is well marked for the Saints Way. Head into the field and walk with the hedge on your right. At the corner of the hedge, walk forward across the field, to the stile in the hedge on the other side of the field. Climb over the stile and walk straight across the next field, veering left, to the next stile. In summer this path is clear through the crops, in winter it is usually quite clear in the earth.

6.   Crossing this second stile you are now on a well-tarmacked lane, and this is where we part from the Saints Way. Turn left and follow the lane down to the main road, which can be busy. This is a private lane and whilst the landowner is happy for walkers to be on this stretch it is worth remembering that this is not a natural right of way.

There is now an option to explore *Castle Dore*. If you don't fancy this, go to Step 9. Steps 7 a-c, go to Castle Dore via the busy road, but avoiding some potential cattle. Steps 8 a-c, go via hilly fields avoiding the fast road.

7a.   As the private road joins the main road turn right and walk half a mile to the next junction. This is the main Golant Road, it's narrow without footpaths and

 St Sampson Church: St Sampson was born in Wales c. 485 AD. In 521, as a Bishop, he decided to go on a pilgrimage to Cornwall. It is believed that he lived in a cave overlooking the River Fowey below where the church now stands. The cave had previously been the home of a dragon that was terrorising the villagers, and seeing their plight, he slew it for them. Having rid the village of this dragon, the parishioners built a church in his name in thanks. Alternatively, Sampson felt the village needed a monastic settlement and built one himself.

If you go into the church, see if you can find the dragon carved into the end of one of the wooden benches, or in the stained glass windows. To the left of the church porch, is an old holy well. It is said that St Sampson, faint from fasting one day, prayed for water and a spring arose. It is more likely though, that this well predates the church, as many churches were built near or on the sites of existing places of worship. Springs and wells have been sites of ancient Cornish worship all across the county.

can be busy, that said cars tend to drive slowly along it. When you get to the T-junction, turn right.

7b. You are now on the main Fowey – Lostwithiel Road. This road is busy and fast without a footpath, take care. Walk along it for 400 metres and then turn right, into the drive of Lawhibbet Farm. After about 50 metres go through the gate on your right and explore Castle Dore. It is on private land, but the owner allows access. There can be cattle in the castle.

7c. Return the way you came. Go to Step 9.

8a. As the private road joins the main road, turn right and walk about 100 metres. On your right-hand side is a stile and footpath sign. Head over it and into the field. There may be cattle in these fields.

8b. Once in the field, you should walk directly across it, navigating an electric fence. You are heading towards the white farmhouse you can see ahead of you, on the other side of the dip. Walk through this field, through the gates and into the field directly below the farmhouse. This is a large field on a downhill slope. Walk towards the fence and gates that you can see below the farmhouse. At the bottom of the field, there are two metal gates, head through these and walk along the hedge on your left. At the edge of the field, turn right and walk up the field towards the farmhouse. At the top of the

Church Gates: After her marriage to King Mark, Iseult gave a cloak to the church, in thanks for blessing her marriage. The lovers' gate at the front of the church is said to mark the spot where Iseult stood and looked out for Tristan. Trees currently block the view of the river, but there are spots in the graveyard where you can overlook the river, and imagine Iseult standing in the wind, her marriage cloak blowing about her as she watches to see if her lover is returning.

Saints Way Path: During the early spread of Christianity from Ireland and the Scottish communities, there was a lot of traffic along the western edge of the British Isles. Saints travelled between Scotland, Ireland, Wales, Cornwall and Brittany. There is evidence all over Cornwall of the impact that the saints had on the land; there are more saint place names in Cornwall than anywhere else in Britain. These holy men and women were clearly passing through Cornwall and whilst an actual path was never known, one could be

field, you will see a gate with a yellow sign marker on it. Go through the gate and onto a driveway.

8c. Follow the private drive through Lawhibbet Farm and head along until you are within sight of the main road. Go through the gate on your left and explore the earthworks of Castle Dore. It is on private land, but the owner allows access. There can be cattle in the castle. Return the way you came. Go to Step 9.

9. Where the private road joins the main road, cross over and head down the lane on the other side. Follow this lane until it turns sharp left. This is where you turn right onto an unmade lane. Follow this lane downhill, and when it turns left continue for a few hundred yards until you come to a gate post. To the right of the gate is a narrow path. Head down this path.

10. This path is very clear to follow but can be extremely wet and muddy as it cuts between fields and woodland. After prolonged rain, this can only be done in wellies. The path leads on to a lane by a farm holding. Walk along this lane.

11. This is the rest of Penventinue Lane that you were on at the start of the walk. After a short while, you will find yourself back at the point when you first turned off. Now simply retrace your route back to the car park.

guessed at. In the late 1990s, a Saints Way across Cornwall, connecting important religious sites from the fifth century, was established. Of course, it wouldn't just have been Saints using these paths. Cornwall was rich in tin, which had fuelled the Bronze Age and there is evidence of the tin trade stretching as far as the Phoenician trading routes. Ireland and Wales were also rich in gold so there would have been many merchants. One story claims that Joseph of Arimathea came to Cornwall to trade in tin and that one of his companions was Jesus himself. Whilst the legitimacy of this claim is weak, the fact that the story exists, lends evidence to the importance of Cornwall, as a place of great resources and international trading for the last two thousand years.

 Castle Dore: Castle Dore is an Iron Age hill fort believed by some to have been home to King Mark of Cornwall a historical figure born c. 480 AD who also appears in the Arthurian myths. Facts from this period of history are very few and far between, and in between the facts, live some great stories. The

EARTHWORKS AT CASTLE DORE

LOST LANES

best of these is the tale of Tristan and Iseult.

Castle Dore was also the site of the Earl of Essex's defeat in 1664, during the English Civil War. He took his army into the west country hoping to secure it for Parliament and whilst Devon and Dorset had some sympathy for the cause, there was very little support in Cornwall. Essex misjudged the mood of the county and realised he was in trouble. He took refuge at Castle Dore overnight but realised that his own army couldn't be trusted and so he fled. This disastrous campaign led to the end of his military career.

LINKS:

Castle Dore http://bit.ly/2G1qQ4N
Tristan and Iseult - Kneehigh http://bit.ly/2GQfO3n
Tristan and Iseult - other versions
https://en.wikipedia.org/wiki/Tristan_and_Iseult
The Old Sawmills http://theoldsawmills.co.uk/history/

PHOTO ALBUM:

https://flic.kr/s/aHsksDCvSe

5

ETHY WOODS

LENGTH: 5 miles
EFFORT: Moderate
TERRAIN: Riverside footpath and fields. The top fields can be very muddy
FOOTWEAR: Walking boots
LIVESTOCK: The top fields often have cattle in them
PARKING: Lerryn car park. PL22 0PT
WCs: Lerryn
CAFÉ / PUB: The Ship Inn, Lerryn
OS MAP: 107

BRIEF DESCRIPTION: A riverside walk that moves inland, passes through fields along the front of Ethy House and back down into the village.

This walk can be linked with Walk 6, Lerryn – St Veep.

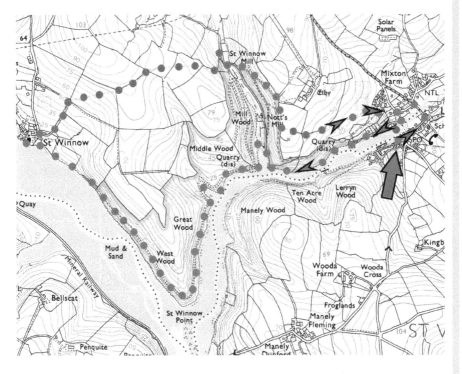

Elevation Profile

200ft								
130ft								
66ft								
0.0ft								
0.0mi	0.62mi	1.2mi	1.9mi	2.5mi	3.1mi	3.7mi	4.4mi	4.9mi

DIRECTIONS:

1. From the Lerryn car park, if the stepping stones are visible, cross the river here. If not, then exit the car park onto the road, turn left, walk along the road and head over the bridge. Shortly after the bridge take the first turning on your left, walk to the end and at the T-junction turn left towards the river. You are now looking over to your car park.

2. Turn right and walk along the river. At first, this is a tarmacked road, but gradually the surface deteriorates as the houses thin out until you get to the entrance to the National Trust Ethy Woods. The woodland path hugs the river for about two and a half miles until it gets to St Winnow. It's very clearly laid out and whilst it can be muddy at times it is mostly easy underfoot.

3. The first section of this river path towards the tiny hamlet of St Winnow is nice and easy. You will pass a mediaeval stone pillar and down to the left of it is the remains of an old quay with stone steps leading into the water. This won't be visible at high tide. Follow the path right and then cross over the creek, do not take the uphill, inland path.

4. Carry along the path, across another creek and soon the path will join an unmade road. Walk along the road, after

Lerryn: The first written evidence of the existence of the village of Lerryn is in the Assize Roll of 1284. The name probably comes from the Cornish word 'lerion' meaning waters. In 1573 Queen Elizabeth I ordered that a rate be levied for rebuilding the bridge in order to aid production of silver.

CELTIC CROSSES

a while, there is a clear turning off to the left. This is a narrow footpath that continues for about a half-mile before rejoining the unmade road. It is closer to the river and more atmospheric but not as easy to walk. Choose either path.

Keep left, following the river until the path ends at a stile. Over the stile and walk along the field keeping the hedge on your left side, over another stile and continue to walk forwards. At the next corner, cross the stile and a small wooden bridge. You are now on the creekside, walk along the edge until you get to the slipway. During high tide, you might get wet feet, and during a very high tide, it might be impassable. Check ahead. Across the river lies Lantyan and on the sandbanks between these two points, the legendary Tristan killed King Morholt.

Walk up the slipway and follow the footpath through the churchyard. Walk out through the second church gate, past the house and turn right along the public footpath. Go through the metal gate and then the track banks uphill and to the left, pass through another gate and continue uphill.

At the top of the track there are a jumble of gates. Walk forward to the gate with a yellow arrow on it, and a stile beside it. Climb over the stile into the field. This is the first of six fields. Cross field #1 on a diagonal path bearing left, you are

ETHY MILL

heading towards a gate on the other side of the field. Pass over the double stile, beside the gate into field #2, turn left keeping the hedge on your left all the way to the next gate in the field corner. Climb the stile into field #3. Walk diagonally across the field heading right, the stile here is often very muddy. Once in field #4 walk across the middle of the field on a left downhill slope. Ignore the gates to your left and right, and soon you will see a gate in the corner ahead of you. Climb over the double stile beside the gate into field #5. Walk along the field edge keeping the hedge on your left, halfway down you will reach a stile on your left. Head over it into field #6. Walk down this steep field keeping the hedge on your right. Halfway down, cross the stile on your right, down steps and onto a lane.

8. At the lane turn right and walk downhill, you are now at Ethy Mill and back on the Ethy estate. Cross the stream and head back uphill. As the trail veers right and downhill, take the path on your left and climb up into the woods. Keep to this path all the way to the top ignoring any left or right-hand turnings.

9. At the top, head through the gate, turn right and walk towards the small copse of trees across the field. As you get to the hedge in front of the trees, turn left and walk down to a break in the hedge. Walk through and continue downhill, with

King Morholt: King Morholt was an Irish king, and Uncle to Iseult, demanding a tribute from King Mark, Morholt wanted every boy and girl aged 15, to be given to him to take to Ireland. Tristan was having none of this and challenged King Morholt on behalf of his Uncle. The battle took place on a sandbank island between Lantyan and St Winnow where Tristan successfully slew the King but not before Morholt cut him with a poisoned blade. Tristan was close to death and, with much grieving, King Mark and all his subjects put the hero, Tristan, in a boat and pushed him out to sea. Tristan's boat floated to sea where he was found by Irish fishermen. No one knew who he was and so he was given to Iseult to heal. Thus she fell in love with Tristan not knowing he was her Uncle's killer and her future husband's nephew.

For more on this legend read Walk 4, Walking with Saints.

THE RIVER FOWEY

the hedge now on your left, until you get to two gates. Ignore the gate to your left and head through the one in front of you. You are now in a very long field, walk forwards heading towards the rooftops and chimneys of some houses, the large house to your left is Ethy House.

10. There is a footpath to the right of these properties. At this point you are now at the top of Lerryn, follow the lanes back down to the river and car park.

LINKS:

Lerryn http://lerrynhistory.co.uk/index.cfm
Tide Timetables https://bit.ly/2IOJw9I

PHOTO ALBUM:

https://flic.kr/s/aHsmfP4tkB

6

LERRYN – ST VEEP

LENGTH: 4 miles
EFFORT: Moderate, one very steep hill
TERRAIN: Footpaths, fields, lanes. Occasionally the path gets very close to a steep bank and you may want to keep children close to you
FOOTWEAR: After heavy rain, the top fields can be wet and muddy
LIVESTOCK: Some potential
PARKING: Lerryn car park. PL22 0PT
WCs: Lerryn
CAFÉ / PUB: The Ship Inn, Lerryn
OS MAP: 107

BRIEF DESCRIPTION: A varied countryside walk, through the woods alongside the Fowey & Lerryn Rivers and then up across high fields with river valley views, finally returning along country lanes.

This walk can be linked with Walk 5, Ethy Woods.

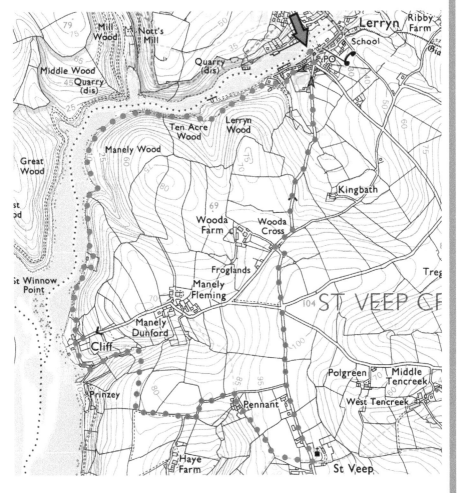

Elevation Profile

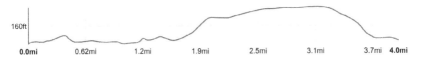

160ft

0.0mi   0.62mi   1.2mi   1.9mi   2.5mi   3.1mi   3.7mi **4.0mi**

DIRECTIONS:

1. From the Lerryn car park, walk up the road past the Ship Inn. After a few houses, there is a footpath sign heading down an alley on your right by a cottage named "Bluebell Cottage". This lane is called Piggy Lane. Lerryn was established to smelt silver so the name could possibly be connected to the pig ore by-product of the process, and not to the fact that Lerryn once had five butchers. Follow the yellow arrows down Piggy Lane and take the path to the left of Woodleigh Cottage down towards the stream. Cross over the stream and take the path uphill and into Lerryn Woods.

Tivoli Park: The Lerryn Regatta was a popular annual event, and at one time it was called The Henley of the West. It was mentioned in the Royal Cornwall Gazette of 1870. There was a break for the First World War and the regatta restarted with a Peace Regatta in 1919. There was a second break for the Second World War, and the regatta restarted in 1953 and ran until 1968 when four thousand people attended.

STANDING STONES

2.   The path here is very clear, as you walk through the first section you may discover the remains of the *Tivoli Park* built by *Frank Parkyn*. Some structures are hidden in the undergrowth, but the massive fountain is more obvious. After the fountain, the path continues until it gets to a gate. Walk past this and follow the yellow arrow post towards the *River Lerryn*. The path by the river is narrow but clear all the way along; it is a lovely walk and lasts for about two miles. Sometimes it veers inland, and other times it goes right to the edge of the river bank with a sudden drop below. Small children should not run ahead when the path edges along the riverside and care should be taken where you walk in case of a path collapse or river erosion. Sometimes the path cuts across a pill or alongside the edge of a creek. The word pill is derived from the Cornish "pyll", meaning creek. Many of the smaller creeks in Cornwall are called pills and the two words are often used side by side.

During a high tide, this section of the path will be impassable, and you will have to turn inland for a few hundred metres before re-joining the path. Check your *tide timetable.*

3.   Towards the end of this stretch, you can see across the river to the point where the Lerryn and Fowey Rivers join, and on the corner a small white building.

Frank Parkyn, one of the members of the regatta committee and a successful miner, bought some woodland on the south of the river from the Rashleigh Estate in 1911. In about 1920 most of the trees were cut down, and Parkyn started construction on a pleasure ground named Tivoli Park after the Tivoli Gardens in Copenhagen which he had visited. The park featured fountains, a pond, a cascade, obelisks, a plunge pool and bandstand. It played a central role in subsequent regattas housing a fun fair, field sports and a pavilion. It has now become overgrown but remains of the plunge pool and large fountain can still be seen.

PARKYN'S FOUNTAIN

45

This is *Penquite Quay*. During summer the tree canopy may obscure your view.

4. Continue up and around a private *waterside residence*, and soon the path will end at a rickety stile by a concrete shed. Climb over the stile and follow the path across a private driveway to a road, you are now in the hamlet of Cliff. Turn right and walk along the road until it ends at Cliff Pill.

5. There is a clearly marked footpath sign heading left, uphill along a stream, follow this path until it opens up into a wild pasture. The fingerpost for this field is currently missing. Walk along the stream for a short distance but then you need to turn right and head uphill toward the middle of the two trees. Between them are a few steps in the hillside. Use these as your guide. Walk up the field following the direction of the steps. As you get to the top of the field, you will eventually see a stile on the horizon, off to your right, head towards this. Be aware that this section is brutal but short. You will lose the will to live, but you may like to reward yourself with the knowledge of spectacular views from the top. I'd like to tell you these will include dragons flying overhead but in all likelihood it will be the next rainstorm! Either way, when you get to the top of the field cross the stile in the fence. If you look behind you, you can see the river valleys, ahead the village you can see is Golant.

River Lerryn: The river has always been tidal and used to be deep enough for barges to carry lime from the Lerryn Lime Kilns down to the deepwater port at Fowey. The *lime kilns* are still visible, but now the river is mostly silted up. There are two ways to cross the river, at low tide and on foot you can cross via the stepping stones or during high tide you can cross via the Elizabethan road bridge. The bridge was mentioned in 1535 and is a listed Grade II* structure.

At times you can be fooled into thinking the river is flowing inland. This is just the strength of the tide flowing in.

Waterside Residences: Lots of properties in Cornwall are only accessible via foot or boat. Some are even further from a road than this one, but all have the advantage of stunning views and perfect isolation, whether it's by the river or sea.

ON THE BANKS OF THE LERRYN RIVER

PENQUITE QUAY

6.   When you have finished looking around or allowing your lungs to recover, walk directly across the next field heading towards a large tree on the left. Keep walking across the field until you get to the left-hand corner. There is a sheep *stile* in the hedge, climb over it and turn left. This type of stile is known as a sheep stile because they can't jump up or over them. Walk along with the hedge on your left, when you get to the gate head into the next field and now keep the hedge on your right. Effectively you are still walking in a straight line, but you have swapped over fields. At the bottom of this field leave through the metal five-bar gate and out onto a road.

7.   Turn left onto the road and walk until you reach a footpath post pointing left and right by a house. Take the right-hand path and follow the white arrows. Be aware that the path now cuts through a private garden and orchard. Head through two white picket gates, through the small orchard and then back into a field.

Penquite Quay: This quay and house were built by Frank Parkyn as an addition to his country home, Penquite. He clearly admired Italian architecture, as can be seen here and in the Tivoli Park, and he was also great friends with Mussolini. Parkyn was a well-connected man and another of his friendships was with the Prince of Wales, later King Edward VII. The Prince visited regularly and enjoyed a bit of privacy at the Quay House with various young ladies. There was also a private plunge pool behind the ornamental bridge, although this is now a ruin. Today the quay can only be accessed by boat as a railway line cuts it off from the rest of the land, and it is a haven for adders.

GLORIOUS VIEWS

8.   Continue, on a straight line towards a gate and into the next field. Here, walk straight ahead, towards the trees in front. When you get to the trees, enter the field on your left, and walk towards the church tower with the hedge on your right. When you see the stile in the hedge on the opposite side of the field, head towards it and cross over. Then follow the path to the church, go through the gate and out onto the road in front of the church.

St Veep Church is a pretty, squat, little church and worth a brief visit. If you are lucky enough, you may hear the *Maiden Bells* ringing.

9.   Once back on the road, facing the church, turn left, this is the road back to Lerryn. It is roughly 1 mile and clearly signposted all the way back to the village and the start of your walk. It's a quiet road, but there are no footpaths, so attention is required. However, it's lovely and downhill.

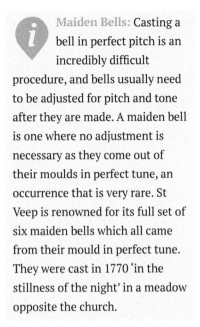

Maiden Bells: Casting a bell in perfect pitch is an incredibly difficult procedure, and bells usually need to be adjusted for pitch and tone after they are made. A maiden bell is one where no adjustment is necessary as they come out of their moulds in perfect tune, an occurrence that is very rare. St Veep is renowned for its full set of six maiden bells which all came from their mould in perfect tune. They were cast in 1770 'in the stillness of the night' in a meadow opposite the church.

LINKS:

Frank Parkyn https://bit.ly/2DPtyYY
Lerryn http://lerrynhistory.co.uk/index.cfm
Lime Kilns https://bit.ly/2rdVj9E
Tide Timetables https://bit.ly/2IOJw9I
Types of Stiles http://bit.ly/2G2bL2X

PHOTO ALBUM:

https://flic.kr/s/aHskvnPpNG

7

PAR BEACH – TYWARDREATH

LENGTH: 5 miles
EFFORT: Easy
TERRAIN: Lanes, fields, sand. Can be very muddy in parts after rain
FOOTWEAR: Walking boots, wellies. Trainers fine in good weather
LIVESTOCK: Potential for cows, but avoidable
PARKING: Par Beach car park. PL24 2AR. Free in winter
WCs: By the second car park on Par Beach
CAFÉ / PUB: Milo's on Par Beach or The Ship Inn
OS MAP: 107

BRIEF DESCRIPTION: An easy stroll around the land that featured in Daphne du Maurier's famous book, *The House on the Strand*. The second half of the walk heads through the remains of an industrial era now almost vanished.

This walk can be linked with Walk 8, Three Beaches.

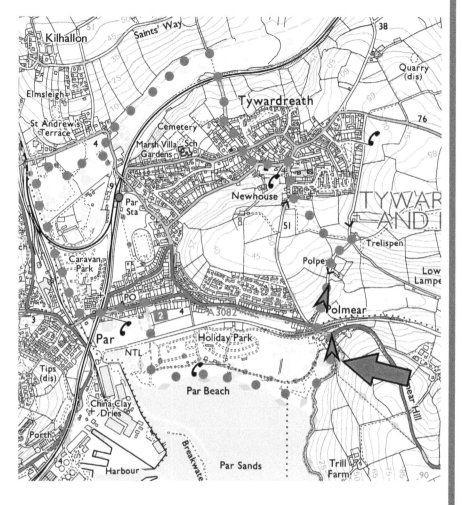

Elevation Profile

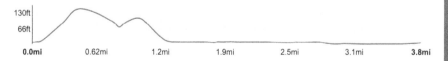

130ft						
66ft						
0.0mi	0.62mi	1.2mi	1.9mi	2.5mi	3.1mi	3.8mi

DIRECTIONS:

1. Park in the first car park on Par Beach, this is 100 yards beyond The Ship Inn, on your left. Leave the car and head back to the main A3082 road, walk a few yards left and then cross the road towards Polpey Lane.* This is a narrow but quiet lane. Walk uphill passing Polpey House on your right until you come to a sharp bend left in the road. Immediately after the bend, there is a flight of granite stepping stones (*sheep stile*) in the hedge on the left. Head up these steps into a field.

If you wish to avoid all possibility of cattle, and / or find stone hedge steps difficult, head up Tywardreath Hill instead, it's the next lane on the right after Polpey Lane. Tywardreath Hill is a narrow lane with regular traffic so walk carefully. Head up it and as you enter the village, follow the instructions in Step 3.

2. Once in the field, head towards the *granite post* in the middle. Beyond this post, on the other side of the field, there are two five-bar gates next to each other, there is a third gate on the far right of the field, ignore this. Go through the right-hand gate and head on a diagonal across the field, towards the wooden fencing in the far corner. Go through the metal kissing gate, down onto the road

Sheep Stile: This type of stile, granite stepping posts in a hedge, is known as a sheep stile because they can't climb them. Although I don't think there are that many sheep in Polpey Lane.

Granite Post: Have you ever wondered why there are often tall granite posts in fields? Rather than an ancient standing stone, they have most likely been installed by the farmer. Cattle like a good itch and can destroy a hedge by constantly rubbing against it, so farmers install an itching post instead. Of course, in the spirit of recycling, a farmer may well have re-used an old standing stone. But not in this case.

CATTLE POST

BIRDS ABOVE TYWARDREATH CHURCH

and turn right. You are now in the village of *Tywardreath*.

3.   Walk along the road passing the large Wesleyan Chapel on your left. At the main road T-junction turn left, towards the Church. Head through the lych gate and have an explore, beyond the churchyard is the possible site of *Tywardreath Priory*. Leave by the second gate heading back onto the main road. Follow Church Street uphill, passing the village hall on your right. As Church Street turns left onto Woodland Avenue, turn right and then immediately left into Wood Lane. Wood Lane is a cul-de-sac, at the top of it turn right and in the corner you will see a signpost for the Saints Way.

4.   Follow the Saints Way footpath downhill; this is a tree covered path that heads downhill and under a railway line. Once past the railway line, if you are walking with a dog now would be a fine time to let them off the lead for a while.

5.   The path now heads into a wild boggy area with a good footpath running through it. Dogs will get wet and muddy. Cross over the first flat granite bridge and as you get to St Andrew's stream, turn left.

6.   The path along this stream can become very muddy, for humans as well as dogs. After prolonged rain, wellies are essential. The stream has clearly been converted into a canal and this would

i Tywardreath:
Tywardreath was home to an important priory in existence from 1088 to its dissolution in 1536 and was rich, powerful and influential. In its day it stood on the banks of a tidal river, as recently as the late 1700s, the tide still reached as far as the village church, but the river gradually silted up. Tywardreath means The House on the Strand, strand being an old Saxon word for beach or river bank. Gradually, over time, through the loss of the Priory and its influence, and the loss of the river as a trading port, Tywardreath became the quiet village it is today. Walking through it though there is plenty of architectural evidence of its former greatness. The only thing that is missing is the known location of the Priory itself, although the best guess places it on the site of Newhouse Farm on Priory Lane.

likely have been done by *Joseph Treffry*. Follow the path until you get to the sluice gates. Dogs back on leads at this point. Cross over the bridge on the sluice gates and continue along the path until it joins a road. Cross this road and take the path on your left by the red dog bin, towards the duck pond.

7. Walk the path around the duck pond keeping it on your right. Head all the way around until you get to a car parking area and take the National Cycle Trail, Route 2 on the left, clearly marked with a blue signpost. Follow the path through the wooded marsh and into an open pasture area, continue until you reach a canal. Turn left and follow the canal until you get to the railway line. Cross the line, this is unguarded so pay attention. Continue along the canal path until it reaches a main road.

8. Cross the road and then head left. Walk under the railway bridge and head up the one-way street. Pass the *Par* Post Office and pub on the left and after a while turn right when you see the wooden signpost pointing towards the coast path. Follow the path along the river, cross over *Haul Road* and then you are into the Par Beach nature reserve. There are lots of paths here, they all head to the beach, so it doesn't matter which one you take, but I like the path to the right as it heads through the pines, for a bit of variety.

i **The House on the Strand by Daphne du Maurier:** This walk is home to the setting of this novel by du Maurier. Part thriller, part time-travel, part historical. It is a very unusual but enjoyable book and lovely to imagine the fourteenth-century landscapes described in the book.

i **Par & Joseph Treffry:** The latter half of this walk wanders through the railway lines and canals that supplied Par Docks and the mining industry. From the mid-1700s, Joseph Treffry developed the Fowey Consols Mines, a collection of various copper mines around Pontsmill, Lanescot and the hamlets above Par and Tywardreath. As these seams ran out, the port then turned to china clay and continued to grow in national importance. The docks are currently in decline and may, one day, become a marina.

Ahead and on the right, you might see the giant steaming chimneys of Par Docks, keep heading in this direction.

9. Whichever path you chose, it will now lead on to the far right of Par Beach. Your car is parked at the very far left end, head towards it either along the road passing the wildlife lakes, through the sand dunes, or along the beach. This is the area's most popular dog beach, and there are always lots running about. At low tide, this is a huge beach and worth walking out on. During extremely low tides you can almost walk out to Killyvarder Rock, marked by a tall metal post out in the bay.

i **Haul Road:** Running between Par Docks and Fowey Docks is a private road. It used to be a private railway line, transporting goods, and is now used for road haulage instead. This is the only point at which you can walk on this road, although it does occasionally open to the public. Haul Road is 7 miles long and also features Pinnock Tunnel which is a mile long; should you be lucky enough to be in the area when the road is open, be sure to go along. Do not be tempted to walk it at any other time.

RAILWAY CROSSING

PAR CANAL

LINKS:

Par https://en.wikipedia.org/wiki/Par,_Cornwall
Railway Yard https://bit.ly/2ufxhj1
Tywardreath Priory http://tywardreathpriory.com

PHOTO ALBUM:

https://flic.kr/s/aHskzVdzLV

8

THREE BEACHES

LENGTH: 4 miles
EFFORT: Easy
TERRAIN: Coast path, beach
FOOTWEAR: Any; footpath can require wellies in winter
LIVESTOCK: None
PARKING: Par Beach car park. PL24 2AR. Free in winter
WCs: Second car park on Par Beach
CAFÉ / PUB: Milo's on Par Beach or The Ship Inn
OS MAP: 107

BRIEF DESCRIPTION: A good wildlife and beach walk, combining three beaches and the coast path. Due to the varied habitats, this is a great walk for *wildlife* spotting, so pack your binoculars. During the summer, dogs are banned on Polkerris Beach.

This walk can be linked with Walk 7, Par Beach - Tywardreath.

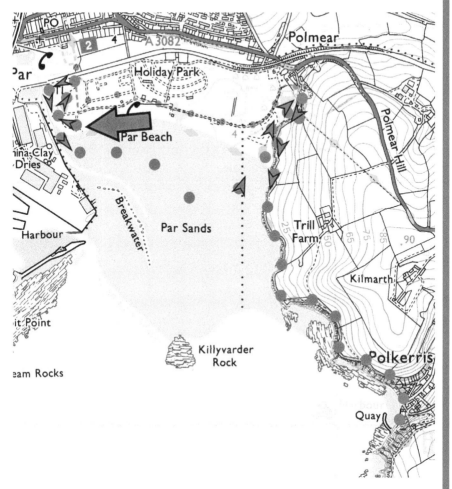

Elevation Profile

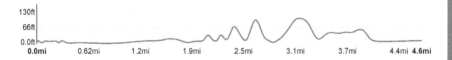

130ft
66ft
0.0ft

0.0mi   0.62mi   1.2mi   1.9mi   2.5mi   3.1mi   3.7mi   4.4mi **4.6mi**

DIRECTIONS:

1. From the main road, A3082, turn into Par Sands. Follow the site road all the way to the very far end of the park, the road ends at a small car park. If the site is busy, park in the very large car park that is to the left of the site road just after you leave the main road. If you park in the large car park, start your walk at Step 7 on the instructions and then once you get to Step 9, head straight onto Steps 1, 2, 3 etc.

2. From the small car park take the clear trail that veers to the right, away from the sea, there is a sea safety board beside it. This trail wanders through a wildlife area, stick to the path. Ignore the first clear left-hand turn that leads to the river, walk on and take the next left-hand turn that leads into the woods. It is marked by a large granite boulder with an arrow on it. Follow the path into the pine woods and continue along as it veers left. Eventually, it will loop back to the path you were just on. Turn right, then right again. Now take the right-hand turning towards the river that you ignored earlier, and walk down to the water's edge. On the other side of the river, the view is dominated by *Par Docks*.

3. Walk left along the river bank until you get to the beach. If the *tide* is too high, head back to your car and walk onto the beach from there.

Wildlife: This walk passes water meadows, pine woods, rivers, dunes, ponds, reed beds, cliffs, woodlands, fields and the sea. The variety of birdlife is therefore very impressive, and we are also lucky enough to have interesting visitors, in winter this area has also been home to bitterns. Out to sea, keep your eyes open for seals, dolphins and, in summer, basking sharks. Otters are also rumoured to be in the area, but they are very elusive.

Par Docks: Par Docks has long dominated the landscape, just as the *China Clay Industry* dominated every aspect of life in this area of Cornwall. It used to be said that if all four chimneys were blowing that they were making money, if only one chimney was blowing they were running at a loss. I don't know if I've ever seen all four blowing, but they may have improved the refining process. It is, however, a declining industry and soon the docks may close altogether.

BOOLIES BEACH

PAR DOCKS

4.   Walk the entire length of the beach. When you get to the other end turn left and follow the footpath by the stream as it leads into a very large car park. Keep following the stream until you get to a small bridge. You should see a sign for the coast path. Cross the bridge, climb a flight of steps and walk up along the coast path.

5.   When the path takes a sharp left turn uphill, you can take the turning that branches off here, down to Boolies Beach. Boolies is a gorgeous beach and often quiet, as it takes a bit of walking to get to it.

6.   Returning to the coast path, head uphill, this section of the path can get close to the cliff edge so best to keep dogs on leads. The path is quite steep, but the views over St Austell Bay are fabulous. Follow the path into woodland and make your way down the hill into *Polkerris*. This is a tiny hamlet with a great pub, restaurant, seasonal café and watersports centre. A dog ban is strictly enforced on the beach between Easter and October, but you can sit, with your dog, in any of the three establishments' courtyards overlooking the beach. Polkerris is very popular in summer and can be very crowded at high tide. It is really lovely though and worth a visit.

7.   Return back the way you came heading along the coast path until you

Polkerris: There are a few places in Cornwall where almost an entire village is owned by one person. Polkerris is one of these places and is owned by the Rashleigh Estate. Its curving harbour wall once supported a thriving fishing industry as well as Napoleonic gun emplacements. It is an idyllic and popular spot and usually avoids the worst of the weather. However, very occasionally in certain conditions, the cove turns into a cauldron.

PAR WOODS

take the flight of steps down into the very large car park at Par Sands.

8.   Now walk across the car park and follow the campsite road as it goes past the duck pond. There are lots of wild birds walking about here, so any dogs will need to be on a close lead. Just past the pond is Milo's, a friendly Italian beach café and restaurant.

9.   On the other side of the road from the café is a path that leads directly into the sand dunes. Take this path and then take the right-hand turning. There are lots of ways through the dunes, but so long as you keep on a straight path with the road to your right and the sea to your left, you will be fine. Keep walking until the path finishes at the end of the dune system and you should find yourself back by your car.

LINKS:

Wildlife at Par http://www.parbeach.com/wildlife.html
China Clay Industry https://bit.ly/2G160GA
Par Beach http://www.parbeach.com/
Par Docks https://bit.ly/2G2GMnf
Polkerris Cauldron – 1825 https://bit.ly/2pzRV8K
Polkerris Cauldron – 2012 https://bit.ly/2HVPwvO
Tide Timetables https://bit.ly/2IOJw9I

PHOTO ALBUM:

https://flic.kr/s/aHsmbfgE9U

9

SOUTH WEST COAST PATH / FOWEY – PAR – FOWEY

LENGTH: 5.5 miles one-way. 11 miles there and back
EFFORT: Moderate / Challenging
TERRAIN: Coast path
FOOTWEAR: Walking boots
LIVESTOCK: Some potential
PARKING: Any Fowey or Par Sands car park
WCs: Fowey, Polkerris, Par
CAFÉ / PUB: Fowey - any, Polkerris - Sam's or The Rashleigh, Par - Milo's or The Ship Inn
OS MAP: 107

BRIEF DESCRIPTION: A beautiful stretch of the coast path taking in lots of little coves only accessible by foot or boat. Walking through Daphne du Maurier country, this short section of the coast path can easily be done, there and back, in a day.

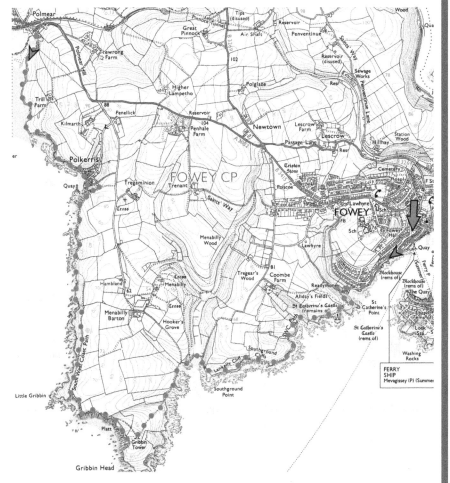

Elevation Profile

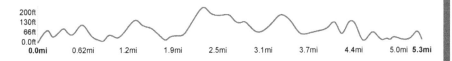

200ft									
130ft									
66ft									
0.0ft									
0.0mi	0.62mi	1.2mi	1.9mi	2.5mi	3.1mi	3.7mi	4.4mi	5.0mi	**5.3mi**

DIRECTIONS:

1. The coast path in Fowey starts at the Polruan ferry crossing. This is one of the points along the coast path where the route is interrupted by a river or estuary. Walk along "Esplanade", away from Fowey, heading towards Readymoney Cove. This is a pretty road but there are no pavements, and it is open to traffic, so take care.

2. As the road turns right uphill, head forwards along Readymoney Road. You may notice signs for the Saints Way as well as the coast path as the two paths currently share the same route. Walk past Readymoney Cove itself and then head up the lane by the blue and white house with the overhanging first floor. As you head up into the woods, follow the coast path signs to the left and walk up to *St Catherine's Castle*.

If you are walking with dogs, make sure they are on a short lead around the castle. Explore the castle and then return to the English Heritage signpost.

3. Turn right at the signpost, back the way you came, and then turn left and immediately turn sharp left and climb a small, steep path up towards the *Rashleigh Mausoleum*. After you have had a look around, head back down to the path, then turn left and walk up to a wooden gate. You are now back on the

St Catherine's Castle: Built in 1538 by Henry VIII to protect Fowey from the threat of a French invasion, it was later modified to house two guns during the Crimean War, and later again, more guns were installed during the Second World War. There is no evidence that the castle defences were ever actually deployed in combat.

Rashleigh Mausoleum: A proper curiosity commissioned by William Rashleigh, a major local landowner. Although his ancestral home was the nearby Menabilly House, he preferred sea views. The Mausoleum sits at the top of St Catherine's Hill overlooking in one direction, the mouth of the Fowey and out into St Austell Bay, and in the other, back towards Point Neptune, the Italianate villa he built for himself.

The Rashleigh Family: This section of Cornwall is utterly dominated by the Rashleigh Estate. Whether it's Point Neptune, the Mausoleum,

POLKERRIS

coast path. Nearly everything of note on this walk is down to the *Rashleigh Family*.

4.   In the distance is a large red and white tower, this is the *Gribben Daymark*. Dogs can happily roam along this section, but after you pass Coombe Haven, you will go through a gate warning about cattle. The next three fields might have cattle in them so dogs on leads until you are certain. The coast path also runs close to cliffs so again, dogs on leads. In the third field, it is easy to see if there are any cattle and the path heads inland, away from the cliffs and towards the woods.

5.   The path now heads into the trees and sharply downhill to Polridmouth Beach. As you walk down, you can see a

Gribben Daymark, the village of Polkerris, Charlestown Docks (just beyond this walk), Menabilly, the Rashleigh Inn, or the Waymarker Crosses; the Rashleighs have built it, owned it or developed it. The family rose to power and riches in the Tudor period, settled in the Fowey area, and were no doubt instrumental in the sacking and reallocation of the Tywardreath Priory wealth. They grew their wealth in shipping and mining, and by 1873 Jonathan Rashleigh was the largest landowner in Cornwall.

house sitting by a large ornamental lake. This was the inspiration for the boathouse in *Rebecca* by Daphne du Maurier.

6. As you leave Polridmouth Beach, the path starts to climb steeply up to the Gribben Daymark, this is the toughest part of the walk, but the views at the top are spectacular.

7. Continue along the coast path but be aware the path is very high here and at times, close to the edge, so keep dogs on leads. Eventually, the path heads inland above Polkerris and then zigzags down through the trees. This is a lovely place to stop, it is very much a local jewel but can become unpleasantly crowded in August.

8. The coast path continues behind the Rashleigh Inn car park and up lots of steps until you get to the top of the woods and into fields. The views over St Austell Bay are spectacular and, in clear weather, you can see out to both headlands, the Gribben to your left and the Dodman to your right.

9. The path heads downhill passing the quiet Boolies Beach before continuing onto Par Sands where it leads into a very large car park. From the site road turn right to visit the Ship Inn or left to Milo's café and restaurant.

Gribben Daymark: "Erected by Trinity House 'for the safety of commerce and the preservation of mariners' the tower pinpoints the approach to Fowey's narrow and rocky harbour entrance. This meant that sailors did not mistake the treacherous shallows of St Austell Bay for the deep waters of Falmouth Harbour." National Trust.

Its decorative design is down to the request of the Rashleigh landowners. This is often open one day a week during summer and is well worth visiting as you can climb all the way to the top and the views are spectacular. Dogs not allowed.

Rebecca by Daphne du Maurier: "*Last night I dreamt I went to Manderley again.*" Hidden in the woods, behind the ornamental lake stands Menabilly House, the Rashleigh ancestral home, that serves as the inspiration for Manderley in *Rebecca*. When du Maurier first discovered the house, it was neglected and probably most resembled the wreck that it becomes in her book. *Rebecca* is a sinister, dark novel but is also a

10. At this point you have walked 5.5 miles. There are good bus links back to Fowey, just head onto the main road by the Ship Inn and wait for a bus, about one an hour. Otherwise, walk back the way you came. Be aware that if you are thinking of walking the main road back, it is very busy, narrow in parts and has almost no pavement. It is not a safe road to walk.

paean to a house. Happily, a few years later she was able to lease Menabilly from the Rashleigh family, restoring it to its former glory, and lived there for twenty-six years.

VIEW FROM THE DAYMARK

LINKS:

Daphne du Maurier https://bit.ly/2DQdsyq
Gribben Daymark https://bit.ly/2pAFf0M
Rashleigh Mausoleum https://bit.ly/2BUN2in
St Catherine's Castle https://bit.ly/2G31gMM
The Rashleigh Family https://bit.ly/2pz0pw0

PHOTO ALBUM:

https://flic.kr/s/aHsmbfgQFf

10

GRIBBEN HEAD

LENGTH: 5 miles
EFFORT: Moderate
TERRAIN: Coast path, fields and lanes
FOOTWEAR: Trainers. Boots when muddy. This is a very popular route and can become quite churned up after heavy rain
LIVESTOCK: Pretty low likelihood, although you do walk through a farmyard
PARKING: Coombe Farm National Trust car park. PL23 1HW
WCs: Steep diversion off the path to Polkerris
CAFÉ / PUB: Small but steep diversion off the path to Polkerris
OS MAP: 107

BRIEF DESCRIPTION: An excellent walk combining the coast path and the Saints Way. A nice circular loop with great views passing the Gribben Daymark.

This walk can be linked with Walk 11, Lankelly Loop.

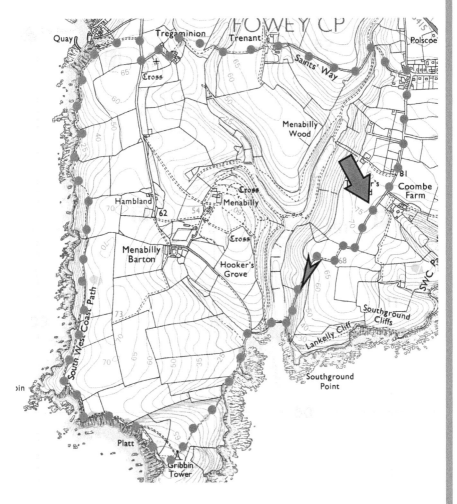

Elevation Profile

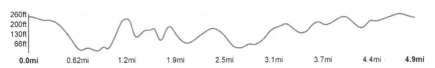

DIRECTIONS:

 1.   Go through the small five-bar gate in the corner of the car park and turn left down the footpath. Follow the path until it ends at a large five-bar gate. Go through the gate into the field and turn left. Walk along the edge of the field, pass the first gate and at the second gate, go through it, back onto a clear path.

2.   Follow the path all the way down to Polridmouth Beach. The house by the beach was the inspiration for the boathouse in Daphne du Maurier's *Rebecca*. At the bottom, turn right, you are now on the coast path and will stay on this path for the next 2.5 miles. As you leave Polridmouth Beach, the path starts to climb steeply up to the *Gribben Daymark*, this is the toughest part of the walk, but the views at the top are spectacular.

3.   Continue along the coast path but be aware the path is very high up here and at times, close to the edge, so keep dogs on leads. Eventually, the path heads inland above Polkerris. This is a lovely place to stop and explore and has WCs but it's quite a walk down to it, and of course back up to this point. The coast path turns sharp left and downhill towards Polkerris, but this is where we leave it. Our path continues across the middle of a field,

 Rebecca by Daphne du Maurier: *"Last night I dreamt I went to Manderley again."* Hidden in the woods, behind the ornamental lake stands Menabilly House, the Rashleigh ancestral. Hidden in the woods, behind the ornamental lake stands Menabilly House, the Rashleigh ancestral home, that serves as the inspiration for Manderley in *Rebecca*. When du Maurier first discovered the house, it was neglected and probably most resembled the wreck that it becomes in her book. *Rebecca* is a sinister, dark novel but is also a paean to a house. Happily, a few years later she was able to lease Menabilly from the Rashleigh family, restoring it to its former glory, and lived there for twenty-six years.

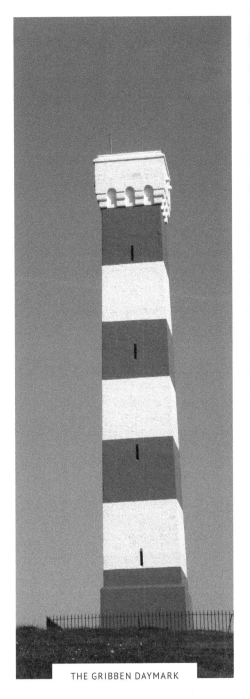

THE GRIBBEN DAYMARK

Gribben Daymark: "Erected by Trinity House 'for the safety of commerce and the preservation of mariners' the tower pinpoints the approach to Fowey's narrow and rocky harbour entrance. This meant that sailors did not mistake the treacherous shallows of St Austell Bay for the deep waters of Falmouth Harbour." National Trust.

Its decorative design is down to the request of the Rashleigh landowners. This is often open one day a week during summer and is well worth visiting as you can climb all the way to the top and the views are spectacular. Dogs not allowed.

although not always signed, the path is usually clear to see on the ground itself, head towards the telegraph pole. We are now walking along the *Saints Way*.

4. At the road, turn right, walk 100 metres along the road and then turn left at *Tregaminion Church*. The churchyard features two *wayside crosses* moved here by William Rashleigh. Now walk down the lane into the farmyard; the path is clearly marked and heads right through the middle of the farmyard. From the farmyard, head into the field, through the gate on your left. Walk down to the footbridge and cross over it into another field. Follow the path until you cross a rickety footbridge and then climb a large flight of steps.

WAYSIDE CROSS

The Rashleigh Family: This section of Cornwall is utterly dominated by the Rashleigh Estate. Whether it's Point Neptune, the Mausoleum, Gribben Daymark, the village of Polkerris, Charlestown Docks (just beyond this walk), Menabilly, the Rashleigh Inn, or the Waymarker Crosses; the Rashleighs have built it, owned it or developed it. The family rose to power and riches in the Tudor period, settled in the Fowey area, and were no doubt instrumental in the sacking and reallocation of the Tywardreath Priory wealth. They grew their wealth in shipping and mining, and by 1873 Jonathan Rashleigh was the largest landowner in Cornwall.

The Saints Way: During the early spread of Christianity from Ireland and the Scottish communities, there was a lot of traffic along the western edge of the British Isles. Saints travelled between Scotland, Ireland, Wales, Cornwall and Brittany. There is evidence all over Cornwall of the impact that the saints had on the land; there are more saint place names in Cornwall than anywhere else in

TREGAMINION CHURCH

Britain. These holy men and women were clearly passing through Cornwall and whilst an actual path was never known, one could be guessed at. In the late 1990s, a Saints Way across Cornwall, connecting important religious sites from the fifth century, was established. Of course, it wouldn't have just been Saints using these paths. Cornwall was rich in tin, which had fuelled the Bronze Age and there is evidence of the tin trade stretching as far as the Phoenician trading routes. Ireland and Wales were also rich in gold so there would have been many merchants. One story claims that Joseph of Arimathea came to Cornwall to trade in tin and that one of his companions was Jesus himself. Whilst the legitimacy of this claim is weak, the fact that the story exists lends evidence to the importance of Cornwall, as a place of great resources and international trading for the last two thousand years.

Tregaminion Church & the Wayside Crosses: Tregaminion Church was begun in 1813 by William Rashleigh, it is now a Chapel of

75

5.　The path comes to a sheep stile and crosses a small lane. Go straight over and continue along the path between the buildings. Walk further until you reach another sheep stile and head straight down the old lane, under a bridge, through a kissing gate and then over a small stream. Now follow the path right and uphill until you emerge onto Prickly Post Lane. Once on the lane, turn right and stick to this road all the way back to your car park.

Ease and rarely open. In its grounds stand two wayside crosses that would have acted as route markers. Just as we follow the fingerposts today, these crosses provided markers for ancient traders and pilgrims. The first, standing by the front porch, is believed to have been moved here sometime in the nineteenth century, possibly from the road outside. The second, larger cross, standing almost complete and off to the side amongst the trees, has had an eventful journey. In the words of Historic England, "This wayside cross was discovered in 1889 in use as part of a footbridge across a stream at Milltown in Lanlivery parish, 6km north of Tregaminion. The head had been reshaped so that it would lie flat against another stone. The monks of Buckfast Abbey, Devon bought the cross for five pounds and moved it to Buckfast. When the landowner, William Rashleigh of Menabilly, heard about the cross, he claimed it and had it re-erected in the chapel yard at Tregaminion, in its present location."

INSIDE GRIBBEN DAYMARK

THE VIEW FROM THE TOP OF THE DAYMARK

LINKS:

Gribben Daymark https://bit.ly/2pAFf0M
Large wayside cross https://bit.ly/2pxXDbk
Small wayside cross https://bit.ly/2pB7nRr

PHOTO ALBUM:

https://flic.kr/s/aHskwB2GXG

LANKELLY LOOP

LENGTH: 2.5 miles
EFFORT: Moderate
TERRAIN: Fields and coast path
FOOTWEAR: Trainers. Boots when muddy. This is a very popular route and can become quite churned up after heavy rain
LIVESTOCK: Cattle sometimes on the coast path
PARKING: National Trust Coombe Farm car park. PL23 1HW. It is possible to join this walk from Fowey, have a look at the map
WCs: None
CAFÉ / PUB: None
OS MAP: 107

BRIEF DESCRIPTION: An enjoyable, short walk, good for dogs with great sea views. There is the opportunity to explore a small Tudor castle and visit the sites that were the inspiration for *Rebecca* by Daphne du Maurier.

This walk can be linked with Walk 10, Gribben Head.

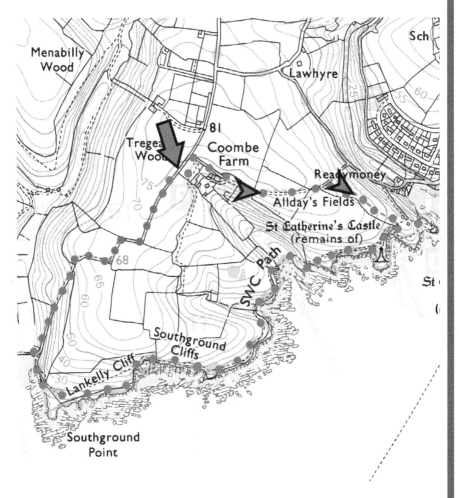

Menabilly
Wood

Lawhyre

Sch

Tregea
Wood

Coombe
Farm

81

Readymoney

Allday's Fields

St Catherine's Castle
(remains of)

St

SWC Path

Southground
Cliffs

Lankelly Cliff

68

65

60

50

40

30

70

75

Southground
Point

Elevation Profile

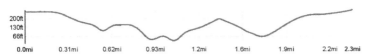

200ft
130ft
66ft

0.0mi   0.31mi   0.62mi   0.93mi   1.2mi   1.6mi   1.9mi   2.2mi 2.3mi

DIRECTIONS:

1. From the National Trust Coombe Farm car park, head back towards the road and take the footpath to Coombe Haven. There is a clear fingerpost, pointing the way. At the end of the lane go through the five-bar gate and into a field. Walk across the field taking the more distinctive path veering left. Walk into the second field and then turn left towards the trees and a black, metal kissing gate.

2. Go through the gate and into the woods. After about 10 yards take the smaller path on the right and follow it down through the woods. It levels out for a bit and then turns left and downhill again, where it stops at the foundations of an old building. Take the steps to the left and head down to a larger footpath. Turn right onto this path and walk to-wards the English Heritage signpost for *St Catherine's Castle.*

i **St Catherine's Castle:** Built in 1538 by Henry VIII to protect Fowey from the threat of a French invasion, it was later modified to house two guns during the Crimean War, and later again, more guns were installed during the Second World War. There is no evidence that the castle defences were ever actually deployed in combat.

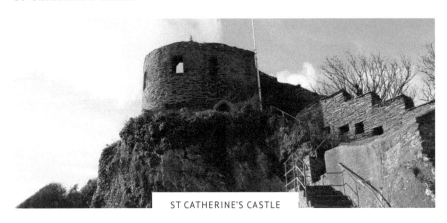
ST CATHERINE'S CASTLE

LOOKING BACK TOWARDS FOWEY'S DEEP HARBOUR

If you are walking with dogs, make sure they are on a short lead around the castle. Explore the castle and then return to the English Heritage signpost.

3.   Turn right, back the way you came, and then turn left and immediately turn sharp left and climb a small, steep path up towards the *Rashleigh Mausoleum*. After you have had a look around, head back down to the path, then turn left and walk up to a wooden gate. You are now on the coast path and will stick to this for the next mile.

4.   In the distance is a large red and white tower, this is the *Gribben Daymark*. We are walking towards it but won't actually walk to it. Dogs can happily roam along this section, but after you pass Coombe Haven, you will go through a gate warning about cattle.

i **The Rashleigh Family:** This section of Cornwall is utterly dominated by the Rashleigh Estate. Whether it's Point Neptune, the Mausoleum, Gribben Daymark, the village of Polkerris, Charlestown Docks (just beyond this walk), Menabilly, the Rashleigh Inn, or the Waymarker Crosses; the Rashleighs have built it, owned it or developed it. The family rose to power and riches in the Tudor period, settled in the Fowey area, and were no doubt instrumental in the sacking and reallocation of the Tywardreath Priory wealth. They grew their wealth in shipping and mining, and by 1873 Jonathan Rashleigh was the largest landowner in Cornwall.

The next three fields might have cattle in them, so dogs on leads until you are certain. The coast path also runs close to cliffs so again, dogs on leads. In the third field, it is easy to see if there are any cattle and the path heads inland, away from the cliffs and towards the woods.

5.   The path now heads into the trees and sharply downhill to Polridmouth Beach. As you walk down, you can see a house sitting by a large ornamental lake. This was the inspiration for the boathouse in *Rebecca by Daphne du Maurier*.

6.   As you reach the beach take the right-hand footpath heading uphill. This section is long and steep, but when you get to the top, you can enjoy the views back down to the sea. Go through the gate and turn right. Follow along the right-hand edge of the field, turn left at the corner of the field and head towards the wooden gate. Pass through the gate, onto the track and follow it until you return to your car park.

 Rebecca by Daphne du Maurier: *"Last night I dreamt I went to Manderley again."* Hidden in the woods, behind the ornamental lake stands Menabilly House, the Rashleigh ancestral home, that serves as the inspiration for Manderley in *Rebecca*. When du Maurier first discovered the house, it was neglected and probably most resembled the wreck that it becomes in her book. *Rebecca* is a sinister, dark novel but is also a paean to a house. Happily, a few years later she was able to lease Menabilly from the Rashleigh family, restoring it to its former glory, and lived there for twenty-six years.

LINKS:

Daphne du Maurier https://bit.ly/2DQdsyq
Rashleigh Mausoleum https://bit.ly/2BUN2in
St Catherine's Castle https://bit.ly/2G31gMM

PHOTO ALBUM:

https://flic.kr/s/aHskwdbi5G

RASHLEIGH MAUSOLUEM

DU MAURIER'S BOATHOUSE

EXTRA HELPINGS

KNOW YOUR TIDES

NB. All figures on this page are rough guidelines. Tides are vastly intricate and complicated, but this will hopefully prove to be a rough but helpful explanation.

The sea goes all the way out and then a bit later it comes all the way in again, and it does this twice a day, day in day out, forever. Whilst it might seem mystical, it works like clockwork and is easily understood, although there is a lot going on.

In the course of a 24-hour day, you will get four tides, two high and two low, each six hours apart. High, low, high, low, high, low and so on forever until the moon falls out of the sky. Within those six hours, a large volume of water is heading either in or out, and it's worth remembering how much power is involved in the sheer volume of water on the move.

Low tides are great for rock-pooling and big open beaches for cricket and frisbees, spreading out and goofing about. High tides are better for boat launches or swimming closer to the beaches edge, snorkelling over rock-pools, or paddling without having to walk ages to the water's edge.

When you arrive at a beach have a look at where the high tide line is. You can easily spot this; it will be a long line of seaweed, this shows how high the previous tide got. Place your towels above this line or be prepared to move them as the tide comes back in. Also consider where you park your car if there are signs saying that a road is liable to tidal flooding, no-one is pulling your leg, and never park on the beach.

The height of the tide is governed by the moon. When the moon is full or new, we get spring tides, when the moon is halfway between full or new, we get neap tides. So, within the course of a lunar month (28 days), we get two spring tides and two neap tides. Spring, Neap, Spring, Neap, Spring, Neap and so on until the world ends. Spring tides, therefore, have nothing to do with Spring, they happen all year round.

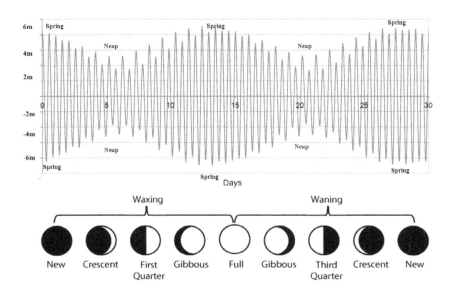

WHAT THIS ALL MEANS

Neap tides give low level high tides and high level low tides. Neaps are normal for want of a better word and provide a nice and easy tidal exchange, up and down, in and out, nothing too dramatic, nice and normal. There is still a large change in the height of water, and the volume of water moving around and still deserves respect and care, but it's nothing like what happens during the Springs.

Spring tides are responsible for high level high tides and low level low tides. Springs are super for all sorts of reasons. Firstly, a spring low tide means that the sea goes a long way out and reveals things not often seen, old wrecks, sunken forests etc., it also means you have access to coves that you normally can't walk to. It is essential that you know when the tide is turning to avoid getting either cut off in the cove or overtaken by an incoming tide. The RNLI picks up people every year left clinging to cliff faces as their fabulous uncovered cove disappears as the tide comes in. And remember it's a spring tide, so it's going to be extra high and extra fast.

A spring high tide is when the sea comes into its highest point, and this is generally when flooding occurs. Most times this is nothing more dramatic than the sea gently lapping into the streets around the harbour in Mevagissey or fully covering the beach at Caerhays. If at all.

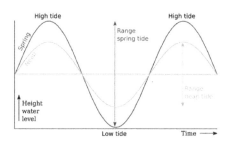

In Cornwall, the tidal range difference can swing between 3 metres and 6 metres depending on springs and neaps.

Major floodings tend to occur when you get a low-pressure system out at sea, (low-pressure gently allows the sea height to rise, a low of .960 allows the sea to rise by 50cm) a low-pressure system usually also brings wind and rain, the wind pushes the waves in and rain fills up the rivers giving the incoming spring high tide nowhere to go. At this point, there is just too much incoming water and it comes in further and higher than the beaches and harbours.

Finally, spring high tides happen around 12 am and pm and the lows around 6 am and pm. Neap high tides are around 6 am and pm, lows at 12 am and pm. Of course, these times apply to Cornwall and will vary in other parts of the world. As the moon moves between full and new and then tides move from neaps to spring the times will also move.

This may all seem confusing and complicated, but it runs like clockwork. If you stay in one location for 7 days, you can see the difference in how the tides behave for yourself. There's a lot more to all this, and if you are interested, there is lots of information on the internet, start with the Met Office or the Marine Coastal Agency.

So there you have it, easy and like clockwork. All you need to do is look at the moon. Alternatively, buy a tide timetable, all coastal communities sell them.

SEASONAL RECIPES

There's nothing nicer than foraging for your own supper. Here are some of my favourite, and easiest recipes, from the most obvious and abundant foods you can find whilst out walking.

SPRING – RAMSONS

Ramsons are a small leafy spring plant that flourish in woodlands. They are also known as wild garlic, and you can often smell them before you see them. The first thing to emerge are their green leaves, usually in huge swathes, followed later by a small white flower blooming above the leaves. They start appearing in February and March, and are generally gone by May. Their smell is very distinctive; if you pick the leaf and it doesn't smell strongly of garlic, then it isn't ramsons.

RECIPE: *Fry some bacon bits or diced chorizo in butter, as they get close to being fully cooked add the hand dived scallops. Give them a few minutes on each side. As you turn the scallops over, throw in a large clump of chopped ramson leaves. When the leaves have fully wilted, squeeze some lemon juice over and serve.*

SUMMER – MACKEREL

It's going to be tough to catch a mackerel whilst out walking but how can you talk about Cornish food and not mention mackerel?

RECIPE: *Chop your fillets into small chunks, dip them in a simple flour and fizzy water batter, shallow fry in oil, dip in sweet chilli sauce. Wonder if life gets better than this. Best served on a secluded beach over a campfire eating the fish you have just caught.*

Alternatively, bake the whole fish in foil and serve with gooseberry sauce.

AUTUMN – BLACKBERRIES

Beyond the obvious, eat as you walk and don't eat the ones below knee height (dog wee), there are loads of things to do with black-berries. They aren't as big or as sweet as the commercial ones, but a perfect sun-ripened blackberry is a total joy.

RECIPE: *Blackberry and apple crumble. If you are lucky enough to find a wild apple tree so much the better, otherwise grab a cooking apple. Chop and stew down with the blackberries, some cinnamon and a bit of sugar. Place in the bottom of an ovenproof dish. For the crumble weigh an equal amount of butter to flour and ground almonds combined, and sugar. Omit the almonds altogether if you want. Just make sure that the butter and dry ingredients are equal in weight, one third each. Rub them all together until you have a breadcrumb mixture. Spread over the top of the fruit and cook until the juices are oozing up through the crust. Serve with custard and joy.*

WINTER – SLOES

Sloes are a blue-black berry that grow on blackthorn bushes. They grow in abundance along many sections of the coast path in autumn and look like blueberries although they are a lot harder. The bushes are generally tall and form a hedgerow, sometimes above your head and very thorny. They are very sour but given time they taste delicious. Sometimes people recommend freezing the sloes for a night before use, but I've never tasted the difference.

RECIPE: *Get a bottle of gin or vodka and empty the contents into a jug. Fill the empty bottle with sloes, no more than half, add a few spoons of sugar and then fill up with the gin or vodka. Drink the remaining alcohol or make another load. Reseal the bottle. Put to one side, every couple of weeks, give it a small shake. Decant for Christmas and enjoy. This gets better with time so put a bottle to the back of the cupboard and rediscover it in a few years. Decant and consider how clever you are*

RECOMMENDED READING

Reading a story set in the place where you are staying / living, always adds an extra something. When the author describes a scene, you are instantly drawn further into the book. The following great stories are set in the area and benefit from that extra dimension.

Rebecca
Daphne du Maurier

The House on the Strand
Daphne du Maurier

Castle Dor
Arthur Quiller-Couch & Daphne du Maurier

OS Map 107

CORNISH WALKS SERIES

Cornish Walks – *Walking in the Mevagissey Area*
978-0993218033   https://amzn.to/2FsEVXN

Cornish Walks – *Walking in the Fowey Area*
978-0993218040   https://amzn.to/2r6bDtL

Cornish Walks – *Walking with Dogs between Truro and Fowey*
978-0993218057   https://amzn.to/2jd83tm

Cornish Walks – *Walking in the St Austell Area*
Coming soon

Cornish Walks – *Walking in the Roseland and Truro Area*
Coming soon

MORE BY LIZ HURLEY

A HISTORY OF MEVAGISSEY
An engaging and informative history of Mevagissey.

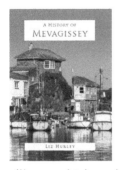

For over eight hundred years, Mevagissey has flourished beside the south Cornish coastline. It was, in its heyday, a globally significant port, lighting the streets of London in the eighteenth century and feeding the homes of Europe. It has been battered by freak storms and a cholera outbreak but has continued, unbroken, contributing in no small part to the colonisation of the world by Cornish men and women.

This potted history gives an insight into the history of the village and takes a humorous look behind the scenes, revealing what it is like to actually live and work in Cornwall's second largest fishing port. It debunks a few myths and introduces some lively, tall tales, as told through local voices.

Available in bookshops.
Paperback: 978-0993218026
Digital: https://amzn.to/2r5VlkA

SCRIBBLES FROM THE EDGE
When everyday life is anything but every day.

Liz Hurley gathers together her newspaper columns to deliver a collection of fast, funny reads. Join in as you share the highs and lows of a bookseller, dog lover and mother in Britain's finest county. This treasure trove of little gems moves from lifestyle pieces on living day-to-day behind the scenes in the UK's number one tourist destination, to opinion pieces on education, current affairs, science, politics and even religion. Watching the sun set over a glowing beach isn't quite so much fun when you are trying to find the keys your child hid in the sand, and the tide is coming in! Join in and discover just how hard it is to surf and look glamorous at the same time. Batten down the hatches as she lets off steam about exploding cars and rude visitors. Laugh along and agree or disagree with Liz's opinion pieces, as you discover that although life might not be greener on the other side, it's a lot of fun finding out.

Available in bookshops.
Paperback: 978-0993218002
Digital: https://amzn.to/2ji2UQZ

LOSING IT IN CORNWALL

The second collection of columns from Liz Hurley, still scribbling away on the edge. Still trying to hold it together. From serious to silly her columns cover all that life throws at us. A perfect selection of little titbits, to pick up and put down or read straight through.

Available in bookshops.
Paperback: 978-0993218019
Digital: https://amzn.to/2r4eHGG

HELLO AND THANK YOU

Getting to know my readers is really rewarding, I get to know more about you and enjoy your feedback; it only seems fair that you get something in return so if you sign up for my newsletter you will get various free downloads, depending on what I am currently working on, plus advance notice of new releases. I don't send out many newsletters, and I will never share your details. If this sounds good, click on the following: www.lizhurleyauthor.com

I'm also on all the regular social media platforms so look me up.

GET INVOLVED!

Join Walkers Talk Back on Facebook, to read about the next book in the walking series. Suggest routes, give feedback, receive advance copies. Better yet, share photos and feedback of the walks you enjoyed.
https://www.facebook.com/groups/841952742623247/

Did you enjoy this book? You can make a big difference.

Reviews are very powerful and can help me build my audience. Independent authors have a much closer relationship with their readers, and we survive and thrive with your help.

If you've enjoyed this book, then you can leave a review on Goodreads.

If you read it online leave a review on the site where you purchased it

Thanks for helping.

Lightning Source UK Ltd.
Milton Keynes UK
UKHW02f1543180518

322842UK00008B/126/P